THE DRAG GOSPEL OF QUEER JESUS

Chris Watkins

Distributed by Independent Publishers Group
Chicago

Please direct inquiries to:

Saturnalia Books
2816 North Kent Rd.
Broomall, PA 19008
info@saturnaliabooks.com

ISBN: 978-1-947817-96-8 (print), 978-1-947817-97-5 (ebook)
Library of Congress Control Number: 2025951034

Book design by Robin Vuchnich

Cover Image: *Kiss of Judas* by Giotto Di Bondone.

Distributed by:
Independent Publishing Group
814 N. Franklin St.
Chicago, IL 60610
800-888-4741

more praise for

The Drag Gospel of Queer Jesus

"Maybe I'm a hymn. A song against binaries…" writes this poet and ecoactivist in their new collection. And yes, they are that, exactly. Watkins reveals to us through non-binary body and riverine landscape, the original intention of Earth for her creatures.

– Susan Cerulean, author of I *Have Been Assigned the Single Bird: A Daughter's Memoir*

Chris Watkins's speakers want for nothing because they are in adept, agile hands. Whether the eighteenth-century gender-nonconforming preacher, the Public Universal Friend, this century's pop savants Doja Cat and the City Girls, or speakers closer to the Midwestern and Florida Panhandle homes that shape [Chris's] ecopoetics most … *The Drag Gospel of Queer Jesus* commingle[s] righteous rage and tenderness … [with a] generation-defining vision and vocal range.

– L. Lamar Wilson, Author of *Sacrilegion* and *Prime*

CONTENTS

II
QUEER ECOLOGIES

III
NOBODY IS DEAD

Jesus is a biscuit, let him sop you up!
—Latrice Royale

SAY MARY, THE MOTHER OF GOD, WAS A DRAG QUEEN

Go with me.
It's just as likely as a virgin birth.
So let's live in a world where Joseph
knew it was a miracle
the whole time
and didn't have to be convinced
by any angels.
Let's say he led the donkey proudly
all the way to Bethlehem.
Let's live in a world—
because we can in a poem—
where no one said anything
about the two of them being together
and raising a child, and Herod
only wanted to kill baby Jesus
because he hated babies,
not for any homophobic reasons.
Let's keep Joseph a carpenter
because they work with wood,
but let's give him well-manicured nails.
Let's have Mary teaching
the little Christ all about illusion—
walking on the water, turning it to wine,
and all you can do with a makeup brush.
Let's say in 30 A.D. a girl
painted on a beard
and began his ministry.

I

BORN NAKED

"WE'RE ALL BORN NAKED AND THE REST IS DRAG"

Look me in the eye and call me a fag,
this skirt will still look good on me.
We're all born naked and the rest is drag.

Laugh at my makeup. Point out my bag.
Tell me I'm only good on my knees.
Look me in the eye and call me a fag.

This body was born with the art of the brag:
I'm the prettiest, handsomest, glamorous she.
We're all born naked. The rest is a drag

if you shop in one section, live like a tag
on your least favorite shirt. Spill the real tea:
look yourself in the eye when you call me a fag.

Baby, I'm not your mother and don't mean to nag,
but deep in your pockets, don't you agree
that we're all born naked and the rest is drag?

Then pull up your panties. Pin up your wig.
Put on a skirt, and come follow me.
I'll look in your eyes, fly you a new flag
cause we're *all* born naked, and the rest is drag.

"NOW SISSY THAT WALK" (A CREATION STORY)

In the beginning, God put Adam in Her
shortest dress and tucked
the boy's penis back between his legs.
The first sound was the rip

of duct tape which She used
to hold it back. Then She put him
in three pairs of tights so everything
down there was smooth.

She made up the boy's face,
gluing back his big male eyebrows
with Elmer's stick glue,
and recontouring his cheekbones

so they became a lady's
cheekbones. She stuck long lashes
on those eyelids and painted
the nails purple and pink.

She gave that kittygirl a wig.
Put her in Her heels,
and told her never to wear
anything shorter than five inches.

Still the girl was looking pretty stiff,
pretty butch, which is not to say
not pretty, but she wanted
to turn a look like God's,

so she had to learn how to walk,
how to talk, how to think like God
who does nothing but create
new things from Herself—

she stitched together
the loose fabric of the soul
and created a comely silhouette
which gave the illusion

that she was shaped like God.
And before long she could walk
without stumbling, this girl with new breasts
and a new name—an Eve.

A woman who was real,
who paid the real price for her knowledge
kneeling at the altar
of her womanhood.

SONNET FROM THE CLOSET

There's a tinted revolving door in here.
Every time I come out, I'm still in the closet.
Saw a therapist for all my Lutheran fears—
doused hell's candle, now it's dark in the closet.
Out shopping in heels and lipstick and lace,
got a whole new wardrobe still in the closet.
Watched Nancy Pelosi come on *Drag Race*
and say get to the polls (or get back in the closet).
I travel, am tolerable in most states' cities.
Like the tabernacle, I carry the closet.
The kind of white person white liberals pity.
It's easy to think of yourself in the closet.
Praise Marsha P. Johnson's first brick at the riot,
but we're still in the stone walls of the closet.

THE DRAG GOSPEL OF QUEER JESUS

Blessed be the cross dressers,
the switch hitters, the glittered,
and the glam. Blessed be the limp-wristed
and the woman who lies with woman.
Blessed be those who hunger and thirst
for some for they will get some.
Blessed be butch. Blessed be the touch
of 0 clippers on a fade.
Blessed be the kai-kai makers.
Blessed be shade. Blessed be lashes
and liner and wigs. Blessed be the fags.
Blessed be the fruits. The genderfucks.
The queers. Blessed be *they* and *them* and *theirs*.
Let everything on earth that is consensual
bring honor to the Lord.
Blessed be the safe word
of the leather daddy in his basement.
Blessed be the fashion statement—
the poofy sleeves, the high-rise pants.
Blessed be the lipstick
on every trans girl's lips.
Blessed be hip pads and binders and breasts.
Blessed be ass and everything inside it.
Blessed be puck and all faeries of the wilderness.
Blessed be each genderless bird and tree.
Blessed be anyone who is persecuted
in the name of me for who they are
or the way they dress.
Theirs is the queendom of heaven.

THE SONNET IN DRAG

She's charismatic, mistress of the brag.
Who turns a look like hers? The highest tuck
you could have—you might say she's enjambed. Her wig
don't ever slip. Her lip sync's never slack.

She struts around in five-inch heels and lines
her syllables in red lip liner. Looks
like one of Shakespeare's girls. And boy she rhymes
like he's inside her—thumbing through her book.

You'll want to read like her. You'll want to wear
hip pads beneath your quatrains. Stuff big words
in every line to burst the iamb's brassiere.
To be Elizabethan, queen of bards.

But can you bring it like a bottom from the top—
from the title to your couplet's death drop?

HARDTIMES JESUS

When Jesus came down from preaching
on the mountain, their side hurt like hell,
and their feet hurt like someone'd driven a nail
straight through the bones.
The pills were making their mouth
as dry as if someone poured vinegar
on their tongue—made it as if their nipples
were wreathed in thorns.
The disciples were on Jesus's case again
about heaven (which seemed further away than ever),
and everyone in town wanted a piece of them—
heal this brother, this bone.
Raise me from the dead why don't you?
The world was turning out to be a sicker place
than even God could've envisioned.
So Jesus kissed their mama, hopped on a donkey,
and road into the wilderness. Satan wasn't out there
testing them. In fact, no one was out there.
Just Jesus and the donkey. So they had time
for their body to go through its changes alone,
to love themself so they could love their neighbor.
And not having to care for everybody all at once
made the love come that much easier—
love sweeter and oranger than the carrots
Jesus and their beloved donkey ate all day long.
So much love that the road back into town
started to look like a good idea. They went
to spread a little love around the city,

and maybe you heard what happened to them there—
what we're all afraid will happen to us
if we can't leave good enough alone.

DEUTERONOMY 22:5

There, cramped between verses about thy brother's ass and verses about chancing on a bird at nest, sits this: "The woman shall not wear that which pertaineth unto a man, neither shall a man put on a woman's garment: for all that do so are abomination unto the Lord thy God." I'm not bothered by *abomination*, that is "ceremonially impure," "away from man," "beastly." I am nothing less than a human animal. I have often laid up happily in my tent beside a lake, listening to four legs move through the undergrowth, then a tongue like mine lapping water. It's not like I've never heard archaic laws read out loud before in school, in church, heard the approving grunts and watched the nodding heads of the elders, the young—though maybe I did not always know or care what was going on, sitting in the pew, picking at the upholstery, greened. And it's not like I haven't ever heard the rebuttals: shellfish prohibition in the same rulebook as instructions for the master and the slave. I've heard all of this over and over. So, the thing I find most interesting is "pertaineth" or pertains, from the French, "legally attached to." And before that Latin, "to belong." And before that, at its lingual root tip, "to hold." I hold this dress in my hands. I bought it; it is legally mine. But more, it looks good on me. It belongs. Suddenly, Deuteronomy 22:5 means nothing more than this worn-out commandment: Thou shalt not steal. Don't take this woman's garment, or anyone's. And I won't. Lord knows, I'd never do such a thing. Or else this verse is just fashion advice from the Head Woman in Charge: My lovelies, all of you, remember the world is a runway to heaven for you to sashay. Don't wear anything you wouldn't be happy to die ~~in~~ for.

BURNING HAIBUN FOR THOMAS(INE) HALL'S CROSS CLOTH

After torrin a. greathouse

Sing, godx, of one with many names and forms. Rage for Thomas(ine) Hall, born 1603, Newcastle. Sing of one driven far from home and into war. Sing an epic-sapphic, seraphamic, many-winged song. Sing! Let us learn. Tell how, in those days, comely James I tried to conquer, like a Roman, the entire world. How, when they were twenty-four, Thomas(ine) took a bread knife to their hair and fought in the Anglo-French War. Sing the name Thomas and mean the same. Sing of them marching beside their friends. Sing of fallen bodies in varied forms. And the bullets that are still taking us away. Sing armor over them, over us, like the shining *harnois blanc* of Joan of Arc. Sing their service done, how they put the name Thomasine back on the way one might tie a girdle tight around the waist, shaping the self. Sing them crafting bone lace to earn a living. How it felt like lily petals in their hands. Sing the time in Plymouth England and hearing of Plymouth Rock, boarding a ship to America and signing the name Thomas again. Rage, godx, that we might envision the invasion of an entire continent. Rage for it is also an invasion to throw someone to the ground, to pull their garments down and say, "*This* is what you are." Rage for Thomas(ine) Hall—pawed at in their sleep by three *respectable* women with clean shifts and scissor clips underneath their petticoats. Rage for the soul is not a medical inspection. Rage for the wrists penned as if for sewing. Rage for Thomas(ine) Hall abused by court order so that everyone might know if they could commit the crime of fornication. Rage for one forced down by two men into the wheel tracks of the street—and this is still happening—rage!—how it happened even after 1629 when the Quarter Court of Virginia declared Thomas(ine) "both a man and a woman" who would "go clothed in man's apparel, only with a cross cloth on the head and an apron before." Why does it always take a jury? Rage! Scream, heavens, that even now, we are not safe.

//

Sing, godx, of one [ ] born [

] into war. Sing [ ] sapphic, serapham [

] the bullets [ ] Sing, armor [ ] like [

] bone lace [

] lily petals [

] man's apparel, only with a cross cloth on the head and an apron before. [

] Scream, heavens, that even now, we are not safe.

//

Sing, armor like [ ] bone

lace, [ ] lily [ ] apparel. [ ] Cloth,

[ ] scream [ ] that [ ] we are [ ] safe.

THE GARDEN (A CONFESSION)

Forgive me, someone,
for, once, I scraped my tongue
with my mother's safety razor
instead of shaving my legs.

Forgive the part of me
that still thinks of this androgynous world—
all these trees walking—
as a punishment for Eden.

It has been 25 years
since my first confession.
Forgive me, anyone who can,
for my fallen

obsession with the gender of dirt.
Forgive me, ape-mothers,
who climbed down hairy
from your hoary trees.

Forgive the serpent in me, Eve,
that lies limp
against my smooth leg
and coils in my head.

Forgive me, serpent,
for you are not a man,
only the tool of men.
Forgive me, first mother,

that I went looking
for a garden here on earth
and a white man in a white robe
who said, *You cannot know what is good.*

I know something:
I want to remove all my ribs
the way you did, mother,
and plant them in my garden

so they vine up into poems.
I want no protection
for my heart where it beats
like the bee's wing of my breast.

Forgive me, heart, or don't
but I need to climb the beanstalks
and watch God—
that tree giant—get undressed.

ODE TO POISON IVY

O seventy-foot vine,
mine hairy enemy,
O three-leafed punishment

in my lawn, how long
at the bottom of this pine
have you been

trying to blister me,
trying to climb
so blasphemously toward heaven?

Because you send
serpentine roots, limbs,
tendrils toward my garden,

there will be battle
in the cabbage bed! I am fitted
with the trowel and the gloves

of self-righteousness,
you with your oily
and irritating knowledge,

but first let me ask this
one last time: You feed
the wrens and the warblers,

are so brightly berried
and red-leafed as if
a change could come—

can there be no soothing
between us, weed, no balm
for our noxious and chafing species?

JUDAS KISSED ME

After Leigh Hunt

Judas kissed me when we met
by the darkening roses in the garden,
the soldiers already placing their bets
on my tunic. I knew God could harden
the heart of anyone—your closest friend.
But even after my final prayer had missed me,
knowing I'd be headed crossward in the end,
it still startled like a serpent when Judas *kissed* me.

STRANGER

One morning I woke up to myself, blank faced as the Shroud of Turin—a stranger.
Now, makeup in the mirror—that it is beautiful or mine—can't tell which is stranger.

"Jesus died for people he didn't even know," said the Sunday school teacher.
I'd learned to look both ways already, wouldn't step out in the street to save a stranger.

At ten, I lost my faith altogether, but still feared hell's crater. God's love
was like the surface of the moon—familiar, but nothing could be stranger.

I wonder: was Mary there, rubbing Christ's back in the Garden of Gethsemane,
watching him kneel in the dirt, like she knelt before Gabriel, that stranger?

The day I wept blood from her womb, somehow, my mother knew me. Away
from our manger, she doesn't recognize my high-heeled gait. She sees a stranger.

I tell myself faith is transition. The bread to body transfiguration. Try not to listen
to the pastors who say, *God's chosen family is the church and the rest of you are strangers.*

Maybe those televangelists are right. I hate when my mother calls me Christopher—
that birth name dead as Christ crucified. His name's in me, but it's the name of a stranger.

MAGNIFICAT

I turned twelve
on the road to Bethlehem.
Joseph hasn't known me
long enough to know,
and I was too afraid
to say anything. He is gentle,
but everyone, my husband-to-be
included, thought I was raped
by Roman soldiers—
which would be my fault
apparently—until a prophet
said something convincing
about how "the shadow
of the Most High came upon her,"
the *her* being me. That isn't
at all how it happened,
but I didn't correct him.
I've heard the priests
and the pharisees outside the temple
bad mouthing Leah and Hagar.
So I road all the way to Bethlehem
with only my silence
and this stranger as company.
But now I want to set the record straight:
God isn't a shadow
cast over you. And God isn't a king
or even a man. I think God is that silence
after two women have known each other,

the silence that overcomes the bedroom
before going back to husbands
and fathers and sons who need them
all the time. Of course, I couldn't
say she was the one who's child
I carry. Her fingers fertile with love.
I don't even know how
such things happen. But they do.
And when we got to the inn,
there was no place to stay,
even though it's run by Joseph's
family. They don't want me here.
They don't want a pregnant girl
for daughter-in-law. So I'm outside
with all the donkey shit that covers
the floor of the stable.
There's a lamb who bleats
all night long, and the cow
produces no milk. I am so afraid
I will not be a good mother.
I miss Galilee, and I'm not sure
Joseph knows what to do
or how to pull the child's head
through the birth canal.
I'm afraid I'll never see her again.
That she'll be caught with another girl
and stoned. Before I left, she told me,
fear is the way God asks

if we are there. All day long
I whisper, "Here I am.
Here I am. Right here."
And I try not to be afraid.
I wonder if anyone but the lamb hears me.

THE APOSTLE PAULA

Likewise, I want women to adorn themselves with proper clothing, modestly and discreetly, not with braided hair and gold or pearls or costly garments, but rather by means of good works, as is proper for women making a claim to godliness.

—The Apostle Paul, 1 Timothy 2: 9-10

I was riding toward Damascus
to yell at some Christians and maybe
stone a few uninhibited women
when Christ, that cowboy,

saw I couldn't ride a horse for shit.
Came down as the wind
and whispered, *buck*, in my pony's ear.
The next thing you know

I've had a vision, a conversion.
I've slept in the house of Christians,
and I'm no longer Saul, but Paul.
I know all the Catholic prayers

better than your grandmother.
And still I couldn't get things right—
always telling women what to do
or even how to wear their hair

in church. O ladies of Ephesus,
surely you know that most of us
need more than one transformation
in our lives. Christ set me straight

a second time by putting me in drag.
And I have to admit, at first,
I thought She was crazy,
coming at me with that makeup brush

as if it were a knife, and I the lamb
of sacrifice, then hog tying me in that corset.
But like most prudishness,
I found mine was rooted in jealousy.

Who doesn't want to wear
pearl earrings, gold eyeshadow,
and to speak of beautiful things?
I wanted every bit I couldn't want:

a costly garment, low cut,
velvet, high slit up the thigh.
I wanted breasts and cat eyes,
glue-on lashes, and hair that bumped

the doorframe when I walked
into the room. I wanted to be
noticed by everyone—to glitter
like a stage light at a cabaret.

My whole life till then had been a lip sync
where I kept getting the words
wrong. No longer! Welcome
to the stage the Apostle Paula!

This one goes out to my
Ephesian sisters. I can't ask
your forgiveness for all the pain.
But dammit! I can sing.

LIP SYNC (VARIATION ON A THEME BY CITY GIRLS FT. DOJA CAT)

Boy, this pussy talk meter, substitution of feet. (in heels)
Boy, this pussy talk iambic, staying on beat. (click clack)
Boy, this pussy talk wordless humming in your head.
Boy, this pussy talk the big shit—beauty and death.

Boy, this pussy talk, kitty girl's giving a speech. (uh-hum).
Boy, this pussy talk, she's using her teeth. (chomp chomp)
Boy, this pussy make metaphors wetter than a whale.
Boy, this pussy like a simile ringing your bell. (ding ding)

Don't nothing but a grant make this pussy talk.
Don't nothing but a Lambda make this pussy talk.
Don't nothing but a Lannan make this pussy talk.
Don't bother with the canon when this pussy talk.

Ay, this pussy's on fire, she'll blow up your journal.
The board says this pussy will corrupt your journal.
This pussy is eternal, don't need no abrupt little journal.
Come get down on your knees while you can suck this, journal.

But this pussy's not high art
This pussy's not proper.
This pussy drinks the cheap shit.
This pussy's popping poppers.

This pussy saw Shakespeare playing with her wigs,
Rosalind's Ganymede switching from a switch.

You want this pussy real bad?
Say, "tenured faculty."
I need a close parking spot
and a decent salary.

Got readers cross the page going crazy over me.
Pussy is burning! Open my library!

Boy, this pussy talk English, Spanish, and French. (wee wee)
Boy, this pussy talk even in translation. (coño)
Boy, this pussy talk smoother than Travolta in *Grease*. (hand jive)
Boy, this pussy talk to Sappho, Clifton, Emily. (crown them)

Boy, this pussy talk 'bout how high I am tucked. (that tape)
Boy, this pussy talk—she's on the tip of your tongue. (mine too)
Boy, this pussy make metaphors wetter than a whale.
Boy, this pussy like a simile not a genital.

Don't nothing but the blues make this pussy talk.
Don't need a fucking muse when this pussy talk.
Don't bother with the rules when this pussy talk.
Don't need no phallic fools cause this pussy talk.

CHARISMA. UNIQUENESS. NERVE. & TALENT.

To write a sestina, you need charisma.
Each word needs some glitter, some uniqueness
like a drag queen. And you've got to have nerve
like a drag queen, enough nerve and talent
to repeat words seven times over—the way drag
repeats the shape of a body and turns out a queen.

If you want to strut down the street like the new queen
of poetry, you've got to talk with your hips, that's charisma.
You've got to be quick-witted. Never let one word drag
behind the stanza. It's true, the uniqueness
of a sestina might help, but it takes talent
to repeat yourself and hit a fresh nerve.

It's a lot of pressure. You might get nervous
even if you are some cut-throat pageant queen,
so just remember it took a lot of talent
even to get this far. And with enough charisma,
an old form, like an old dress, becomes the shape of uniqueness.
Exaggeration, silhouette, that's drag.

Don't be shy. Don't end stop yourself. It's a drag
to watch a fierce bitch get unnerved,
and no one's asking for a eunuch,
just a tight tuck—be the queen
of enjambment. Baby, charisma
is makeup, not some God-given talent.

Let blush sweep you up in its talons.
Let a powder brush drag
across your lines. Charisma
is as internal as your rhymes. Have the nerve
to pucker for each syllable like it's a lipstick. Queen,
it's time to lip sync, but make the words unique.

Even with someone else's words, you can be unique.
Yes, to do that takes a lot of talent,
but, baby, you're more than just a look queen.
You're serving mouth, which is drag
speak for poetry. And no one will question the nerve
you have to do anything from sonnet to chiasma

if you make it unique. On days you're feeling uncharismatic,
talentless even, when all those fishy queens are getting on your nerves,
remember: You can wear anything, even sestinas—all art is drag.

II

QUEER ECOLOGIES

QUEER ECOLOGIES (HAIKU AND TANKA)

we've all seen two boy
dogs go at it, but Nature,
you've heard, isn't queer

a farmer said once:
every peacock's a drag queen,
she paints blue bright eyes
in her five-foot tailfeathers
which grow like glue-on lashes

i paddle through marsh
grass till water turns brackish—
both nonbinary

that class project where
caterpillars transitioned
from green lumps, larva,
into swallowtails, monarchs—
and me in my chrysalis

the ruby breasted
hummingbird deep-throated by
cardinal flowers

ornithologists
assigned four genders to white
striped sparrows; turn those
binoculars on me—i,
too, can be scientific

WALDEINSAMKEIT

"[T]he feeling of being alone in the forest, usually a sublime and spiritual feeling."
—*German-English Dictionary*

I'm never more German or alone
than in Florida, walking the Cathedral of Palms—

its midday darkness like *Shwarzwald,* the Black
Forest, the woodland of the Brothers Grimm,

but here blue day is dimmed by the dead
fronds which clatter in the air above me,

and I think (God knows why) that *this*,
this is the place to be alone and not lonely—

treading stagnant water up to my knees,
pinching ticks and pulling leeches from my legs,

I am never more certain that my blood is holy,
more certain fear is a spiritual thing. I have seen

the cotton white mouth of a water moccasin
flash wide with warning and had no one, if bitten,

to lean on out of the trees. I have seen the sky held up
by pillars of palm—all the leaves a Hosanna,

a Psalm. I know what it means to be made up of bone:
to be another kind of trunk in the congregation of trees.

HAWK WATCHING

High up the gum tree
that is not another knob
or knot or net of Spanish moss
weighing down the leaf-bare branches.

That is the red-shouldered hawk
who rules the ditch-land
at the limit of the forest.
The snake-gripper, the plummeter

light as a loblolly cone.
You will have to admit the world belongs
to her when you see how we go on
spinning under her wings,

or listen for the rose thorn of her cry,
air bent to the tip of her beak.
What is it, all day, crossing
and recrossing her mind but death?

Yet she is no carrion thing.
What is she but the justice of the earth?
Her all-encompassing eyes—
like dewdrops hanging

from the needles of the pines—those changeless
eyes, those blood-rimmed eyes, those eyes
of the Christ in Majesty—
surely those eyes are fixed upon me.

HOOPOE GHAZAL

"O people! Lo! we have been taught the language of birds,
and have been given abundance of all things. This surely is evident favor."
Surah 27, An-Naml, Verse 16

Have you heard the hoopoe? Heard her calling
"hud-hud," calling "hoo-pah?" The *upapa epop*—her calling

timbred as a flute? Have you seen, on a branch,
the forbidden zebra fruit, her wings? Heard her calling,

or watched the orange galea bristling from her head?
Bird of the kings, herald of Solomon. They were calling

her trickster, calling her jinn—beak thorned in the crown
of mischief and sin until God heard her calling,

made her wisest of birds. Attar, in his poem, set her off
for the Simorgh. Through seven deep valleys, all birds were calling.

All birds but shadows of the one great unveiling.
All calls but echoes. All words failing. Do you feel your calling

when she's in the field? The name for humanity is no longer
falling when I see her flying, when I hear her calling.

LITTLE RED RIDING HOOD (A RECITATION IN DRAG)

Many who saw him did not like him.
So he took his Elmer's glue and blocked out his brows.
Hidden in the trees, with mother's foundation, painted a true girl's face
over those boyhood features.

With Elmer's glue, you can block out your brows,
but you cannot block out all the words
about your boyhood features.
She pulled her bonnet down over her ears,

but it couldn't block out the words
of her big armed father always trying to butch her.
She pulled down her bonnet. In her own ears
she whispered a plan for the future.

Her big armed father was always trying to butcher
some poor animal penned in like her,
so she made a plan for the future
else she be eaten up by the world—what big teeth it has.

What a poor animal. Penned in like her,
who wouldn't make a break for the woods
else they be eaten up by the world—the big teeth it has
the better to eat you with? They left with some cakes, some wine.

Who wouldn't make a break for the woods
in a world like theirs, like ours?
The better things to eat, they left with—some cakes, some wine.
The only worry out there would be wolves.

In a world like theirs, like ours,
it isn't always safe to stay on the path toward grandmother's.
The only worry out there is the wolves
which are not half so bad as the axe-happy woodsmen.

It isn't always safe to stay on the path toward grandmother's,
so they wandered through the slatted light of the branches
which are not half so scary as the axe-happy woodsmen make them out.
And though I cannot say they were always happy,

they wandered through the slatted light of the branches
where nobody who saw them did not like them.
And though I cannot say they were always happy,
they had the trees, and their mother's foundation, and their true face.

I LIKE TO SHIT IN THE WOODS

because it feels good—
feminine—to squat
over a hole I dug
with my own orange shovel,
because there is none of
this symbol:
versus this one:  ,
because a bear
has never told me:
You do not belong out here,
because mosquitoes
bite my bare ass
the same as anyone else's,
because I, like any other
animal—from blue whale
to protozoa—must excrete,
because behind a tree
is more discrete
and less politicized
than any stall
I've ever entered,
because in the forest
I have no shame
for the bare branch
of my body,
because in the darkest brambles
of the forest
I am not afraid.

DAVINA COCKETT: QUEEN OF THE WILD FRONTIER

After Danez Smith

Let's make a movie called *Davina Cockett: Queen of the Wild Frontier.*
A remake naturally. Remakes are all that ever gets made these days.
This movie will be the 1955 Disney hit starring Fess Parker, except
our coonskin capped hero/heroine, will be a drag queen *and* a wilderness
enthusiast. This will not seem strange to any of the other characters.
What is historical accuracy anyway? Isn't the "American Wilderness" already in drag?

Serving National Park realness, henny! Like the Lone Ranger in those grey tights.
And how was he "lone," anyway, if he had Tonto with him all the time? Which reminds me,
keep Johnny Depp away from this movie. We don't need another 2013 fiasco.
When will Disney learn it has never been a good time to put a white man in red face?
In this version, everyone will be in full makeup, but no one will be in red face.
This is the final frontier for American children's cinema. Think John Waters

meets Sesame Street. We all saw Divine. Davina will be just as hellish and heavenly!
She'll put the camp back in camping. Her and her good Judy Georgina
will kaikai in their tent (a cut to black kind of scene—for the children). And Georgina
will wear a bandana as red as Joan Crawford's in *Johnny Guitar*. Not only will Davina
grin down a bear (pronounced "bar")—that is, to fight it off with only her winning smile—
but she will charm beavers into traps with the flip of her hair (Davina *loves* beavers!).

And she will run down a deer—in heels! This girl will catch a bullet between her teeth, yes,
but she'll also do it without smearing her lipstick. And she will not murder people like it's a hoot.
She will not wrestle anyone to end the Creek War (though maybe she wrestles just for fun).
Davina Cockett will not trust the U.S. government or its treaties or any pieces of paper,
and she will laugh during the scene where Tecumseh spits dip juice in Andrew Jackson's eye.
But this is not a movie to soothe white guilt, either. Thousands of people will die. This is American history.

We'll have to change the theme song, of course, but no need for a complete rewrite.
Something like: "Born on a mountaintop before Tennessee
was a slaveholding state in the land of the free.
She sashayed through the woods, so she knew every tree,
and kikied with a bear when she was only three:
Davina! Davina Cockett! Queen of the Wild Frontier!"

Davina should go to Congress to try to change things. And just like Fess, just like Crockett,
she won't get anything done. People love to watch legislative inefficiency! That's why
C-SPAN is always on.
We'll film a scene where Davina makes an impassioned speech before the empty seats of the Senate
(though Crockett was in the House). She'll storm out of the chambers and ride off to a pointless cause
just like in real life. And we will all know in the audience what is going to happen at the Alamo.
Except it doesn't happen the same way it did in the original. Davina does not go down swinging

her empty musket like a bat as Fess did in 1955—the shot does not fade to black
and immortality. No one whispers in the audience: *Remember the Alamo.* Which reminds me,
this is not a victory for anybody, but the beginning of the border. Cut to present day: birds migrate
over the wall. Cut back: Davina's captured by Santa Anna, the one man she can't seduce. As
she's marched
to the firing range, we don't flashback, don't see the mountain of her birth. She'll never be a child again.
She is a woman, a man, a person, anyone shot standing in a dress, and no one will remember.

AT THE END OF HIS LIFE, NIKOLA TESLA FELL IN LOVE WITH A PIGEON

She'd fly through
the open window of his room
on the thirty-third floor
of the Hotel New Yorker

where he passed the last
decade of his life.
She was pure white
except for the grey tips of her wings

and her red feet. He was afraid
to eat with spoons another person used,
but was perfectly comfortable
rubbing her plumage

with his fingertips and then
with the back of his hand, cooing
to her as he did. He said *I loved her*
the way any man should hope to love a woman:

a love outside mere bodily desires,
a love higher, that stretched
the mind around the soul.
The night before she died

she flew onto his outstretched arm
and began to glow.
She was brighter than any lamp
that would ever be lighted.

CHARLES DARWIN AND I RECONSTITUTE THE GLUTTON CLUB

The Carolina chickadees knock
a shaker's full of seeds
from the fruit of my gum tree.
The little kernels land on our plates
with a sound as small as salt.
Looking up, "The sandwich is good,"
he says. And through a mouthful
of seitan, asks, "Really, no meat?"
"None," I answer. "It's no agouti,"
he tells me and smiles with this—
a leaf of lettuce is stuck in his teeth—
"but surely closer to chicken
than brown owl or bittern."
"How many have you eaten?"
I ask. "Who's to say.
I've tasted most my beetles,
iguanas, armadillos, a puma once.
Giant tortoises were popular
with the men on the ship."
"Was there ever regret?"
I wonder. "Is there any now?"
I don't give an answer,
but I ask him if he's heard
one of his finches is like to go extinct.
"I have," he tells me, shoving fries
into his already full mouth.
"And that one—did you ever eat?"
He puts down the sandwich in his hand,

chews and swallows his most recent bite.
"Love for all living creatures
is the most noble attribute of man—
I wrote that, did you know?"
I nod *yes* to him. "Eating,"
he says, "is disappointingly bestial—
the mind mastered by the stomach,
the mouth no more than teeth."

GLOBAL EMISSIONS ROSE INTO THE ATMOSPHERE LIKE EMISSIONS RISING INTO THE ATMOSPHERE

after torrin greathouse after Ilya Kaminsky after Pablo Neruda

I give up on metaphor and simile.
The fish hawk did not fly like a coat hanger
on which to drape my grievances,
but like a fish hawk.
And her cry was not a thorn
like those pounded into Christ's head,
but the ordinary cry of a fish hawk
with nothing in it of forgiveness.
And mullet swam in schools
beneath her shadow not like
our collective imagination for reducing
the warming of the planet,
but like a school of mullet.
Crude oil spilled into the Gulf,
and it was not the dipping of day
into darkness, but crude oil
spilling into water, and turtles
ate of it because it appeared like jellyfish,
but it was not jellyfish,
and the turtles were overcome
with bleeding and with ulcers.
And the ulcers were not like a red spot on the surface
of Mars, but like ulcers on the lining of the stomach.
And the gas tank in my car was not
like the lining of a stomach, but like a gas tank
that I continued to fill.

And global emissions did not rise into the atmosphere
like prayers rising toward heaven,
but like emissions rising into the atmosphere.
And even hearing it in plain speech,
without symbol or the fruiting bodies of language,
I still cannot bring myself to understand
what we are doing.

ANTHROPOFUCK

World has me fucked up.
Saying, fuck me. Fuck me.
Fuck husbandry.
Fuck being married to the planet—
an abusive relationship at best.
Fuck Adam. Fuck "dominion over the earth."
Fuck your/my birth
right. Fuck "be fruitful and multiply."
Fuck the sacrificial lamb.
Fuck the factory farm.
Fuck fields of amber grain.
Fuck the dust-bowling
settlers of the Great Plains.
Fuck agrobusiness.
Fuck anything more industrious
than a weedy patch of coneflowers.
Fuck a bushel of roses.
Fuck McDonald's Idaho Golds.
Fuck Monsanto
and the round-up-ready plant.
Fuck corn (not maize).
Fuck the 15% ethanol in my gas tank.
Fuck gas guzzlers. Fuck hybrid cars.
Fuck Henry Ford and the locomotive.
Fuck it all the way back
to London's Great Horse Manure Crisis.
Fuck the Deepwater Horizon
hemisphere in our brains.

Fuck "dolphin-safe" tuna.
Fuck grass-fed beef. Fuck recycling
campaigns—the Great Pacific
Garbage Patch is twice the size
of the Great Barrier Reef.
Fuck every green dollar
preventing poor people from going green.
Fuck the lightbulb.
Fuck Thomas Edison
and Benjamin Franklin's slave-owning ass.
Fuck the energy efficient washers and dryers
they sell the middle class.
Fuck Bezos. Fuck Musk.
Fuck every Paris Agreement
billionaire motherfucker giving us
their take-a-penny-solutions.
Fuck me and my moneyed fingers
for typing "fuck the Industrial Revolution"
—and this whole poem—on a Mac.
Fuck poems. Fuck language.
Fuck opposable thumbs.
Fuck walking upright.
Fuck crawling out of the sea.
Fuck multicellularity.
Fuck the lightning that struck the ooze.
If we have to be elemental again,
let's get elemental. My friends,
it only takes a few Carbon

atoms to live. And I want to live.
And I want the birds to live.
And I want the rivers to live.
And I want the glaciers.
And I want the coral reefs.
And I want those chainsaw fishes
to hang their wicked lanterns
in the darkest gullies of the sea.
And I want the world screaming,
fuck me! Fuck me! Fuck me!
But this time, I want it to be good.

ARK

God: Build thee an ark, Noah. A great rain is coming.
Noah: First, I need the oil that will power my ship.
God: Gather thee animals two by two.
Noah: First, I need to make room for all the cows I will be taking.
God: The rain is coming. You must get to work.
Noah: First, I must build this beach resort for I will need money wherever I am going.
God: You must hurry. Time is short.
Noah: First, I must form an international committee.
God: You are running out of time. There is so little time.
Noah: Some species will have to be sacrificed. We cannot rush things. Some people will have to die. Surely you can understand a blood offering.
God: There is almost no time. What are you doing?
Noah: It is more complicated than you think. People's livelihoods are at stake. You can't expect us to change everything overnight.
God: There is no more time. It must be done now.
Noah: It can be difficult to predict the weather.
God: Look at your wet hair. Have you not noticed it is already raining?
Noah: It is difficult to predict the weather. It could stop soon. It is likely to stop soon.
God: It is already above your ankles. You must start building.
Noah: It will stop any time now. Then, won't I look foolish in a boat.
God: It is at your knees. Soon you will be drowning.
Noah: I can feel it lightening up. If we bottle it, we can sell the water.

WATERS BOP

Florida spring waters. Crayon blue waters.
Grab-a-mullet-with-bare-hands waters.
Glass-bottom boat waters. River otter float waters.
Alligator drags! Suwanee cooters and yellow-bellied sliders
sunning on a log. Dolphins swimming up rivers, manatees
breaching by my boat. I am in love with these waters.

I've got peace like a river in my soul.

Nestlé ™ waters. Bottleable waters. Brokerable.
Brokenable. Bared oyster bars and bleached boneyards
of the coral reefs. Climate scorched waters.
Global South waters. Buried aquifers with oil leaks.
Deep Water Horizon seas—oil rainbows on the pelicans' wings.
Glacial melt waters. Great Pacific Gyres. Rising
waters no sea wall can contain. Mangrove-shaved
shorelines split open to the hurricanes.

I've got peace like a river in my soul.

I have paddled these waters. I have swam in these waters.
Are these clean waters? This pipe? This tap?
Whose are these waters? Which country's? Whose map?
Whose lives are worth the waters? Whose bodies
are in the waters? Which species? My body
is all water, your body. I drink. I am dammed.

I've got peace like a river in my soul.

FROM THE BEARGARDEN

"At length a blind bear was tied to the stake, and instead of baiting him with dogs, a company of creatures that had the shapes of men and faces of Christians (being either colliers, carters, or watermen) took the office of beadles upon them, and whipped Monsieur Hunkes till the blood ran down his old shoulders."

—Thomas Dekker 1572-1632

I have learned strange things:
the world is a pit
with raised seating for spectators.
There is the post in the center

and your leg is chained to the post
so you cannot travel the limit
of your world. The dogs
(there are dogs) travel beyond the limit

and intrude on you
like all the thorns of a berry bush.
The world is mostly hairless creatures
who cannot walk on four legs.

They call themselves humans,
or more often than not, men.
They will feed a dog
food from their table.

Sometimes I am fed the scraps of the table.
Sometimes I eat the sour gristle
that is a dog. They are not like a handful
of honey or a fatty salmon.

But there are no bees or fishes here.
There is no deep water
where one could go fishing.
There are no trees.

Men call this a bare garden.
And there is much noise
from the mouths of men:
"charivari, skimmington."

Noises are sometimes names.
I have a name. I have never needed one,
but I am named Harry Hunckes.
A name does nothing for you.

You cannot eat a name.
It is not a hole in the ground
where you can sleep away winter.
A name is not at all like a mother

who will protect her cubs.
It is only a human thing—
brutal or useless.
Even a named dog can be eaten.

VULTURES

the saviors of the roadside, heavenly stomachs where botulism and anthrax no longer irritate, that last great merry-go round the blacktop like chambers of a revolver, shadows escaped skyward—sifting the flesh left beyond the white lines, jawing each rigor mortis joint,

MIGRATIONS

I hear the geese honking
from a great distance,
then see their crooked shape
arrowing up the horizon and wonder how far
they've travelled already, replacing
one another like some protean spell—

on beats the echelon, the rear replacing
the leader who falls back honking
with exhaustion—each wing beat, a great distance.
What intimacy it must take for one to know when another needs a spell
from the squall—even if that intimacy is far
from what we call *humanity*. It shouldn't take the shape

of their arrowhead to point out—it's far
too clear—that we need to replace
our monologuing over the earth, each other. Honking,
they give themselves over to the wing-shaped
wind, carried by solar flares and the climatic spell
above the backyard fences in the distance.

There, all day, they spell and respell
the letter V at the heart of *love*. See how far
they have crossed this continent's alphabet to replace
snow with simple grass. What distance
would any of us go? What seasons shape
our heads' migrations—our thoughts honking?

What seasons? I can't help think what rough shape
we've left their world in. Like we need a spell
to fix it. Need to grow out every human neck as far
as it will grow. To start honking
whole dictionaries and hearing the distance.
Any smokestack thought can be replaced

with clean sky and clear rivers. To close the distance
in our own humanity, can we find bird shape?
Believe it or not, the mind holds such spells.
This out-of-season life is not easily replaced,
but when I hear their chorus of honking,
my ears, then my eyes, take me that far.

APOCALYPSE NARRATIVES

What if this isn't the end of the world?
We just go on wrestling the elephant.
And earth is not some distant habitat.
Death neither abstract nor irrelevant.
The planet doesn't tip, and we aren't hurled
into darkness. If there is some time yet

to save what we thought lost already—whales,
salamanders, ourselves, and the longleaf
pine. Say a bleached boneyard of coral reefs
and God's nuclear winter aren't behind the veil.
            What if?

FLORIDA JESUS

Florida Jesus is in ole' swamp chicken
walking on the water.
Florida Jesus ain't afraid of no alligators.
Florida Jesus died on the baldest bald cypress tree.

Walking on the water
like the knees of the cypress,
Florida Jesus (who died on the baldest bald cypress tree)
extends you a hand like a cabbage palm.

Get on your knees like the cypress.
Your faith is edging on the surface of the river,
extending you a hand like a cabbage palm.
Florida Jesus is blue as that blue water rising from the spring

because your faith is edging on the surface of the river
like a long-legged water skeeter.
Florida Jesus is blue as that blue water. Rising from the spring—
your heart's water is fit for a glass bottom boat.

Like a long-legged water skeeter,
Florida Jesus eats all the mosquito larvae in your soul.
Your heart's water is fit for a glass bottom boat,
Florida Jesus has taken out all the farm chemicals.

Florida Jesus eats all the mosquito larvae in your soul
like a mighty mullet.
Florida Jesus has taken out all the farm chemicals.
But Florida Jesus is also that hurricane bruising the Gulf.

Like a mighty mullet,
Florida Jesus is jolting, jumping out of the river.
Florida Jesus is that hurricane bruising the Gulf,
blowing over a mile of longleaf pines.

Florida Jesus is jolting, jumping out of the river
with a mouthful of swords.
Blowing over a mile of longleaf pines,
swallowing whole islands of mangroves.

With a mouthful of swords,
with osprey talons, clutching a fish,
swallowing whole islands of mangroves—
Florida Jesus is also as still as a coral reef.

With osprey talons, clutching a fish,
Florida Jesus is as meek as low tide.
Florida Jesus is as still as a coral reef,
and Florida Jesus is the great peninsula creator.

Florida Jesus is as meek as low tide.
Florida Jesus is just an ole' swamp chicken.
And Florida Jesus is the great peninsula creator—
Florida Jesus ain't afraid of no alligators.

III

NOBODY IS DEAD

PRAYER (II)

After George Herbert

Prayer—even now, secular,
every poem you write, a knees-bent child
leaning on their mattress. The mouth molecular.
The porno of your guilt. A *Girls Gone Wild*
of the soul. The clear spring polluted
by farm chemicals. A two-way radio
in the internet age with the mic muted
and no one on the other end to know.
A hope, a slipper in a fairytale.
A time to yell at Gods we don't believe.
Christ's old phishing pole. The junkmail
in your head. The easiest way to grieve.
Something you know and never understood
like how faggot means you and love and burning wood.

I'M NOT A ______

After Harold Norse

"I'm not a man. I don't want to destroy you."

I'm not a man. I don't want to fix you. I don't like to fix things. And I don't own a table saw. I call a plumber or an electrician when there are problems with the house. I know the names of flowers better than the names of football teams.

And I'm not a woman. I can cook. I can clean if that's what you are asking. I make a mean Mushroom Bourguignon. But I'm not a woman.

Yes, I have a penis, but a penis is not a man. If it were larger, this would still not be a qualification.

I'm not a woman. Though you can cry in front of me, and I won't call you a pussy.

But I'm not a man either. And I'm not trying to confuse you. I don't like riddles. And I didn't make up the rules about these things. I read instructions carefully, and I'm not afraid to ask for directions.

I'm not a woman. Even if most of my clothes are from the women's section. Even the clicking of my heels on the tile floor is not the sound a woman's heels would make. Even beneath my "She's on Fire" red lipstick—even when I'm craving dick, I'm not a woman.

And I'm not a man, but I have known many good men, and I do not hate my father. I could set you up with someone if you are looking.

I'm not a woman. I'm a momma's kid. I'm a bedtime story. Little Red Riding Wolf. Or Peter Pan meets Wendy. I am a lost boi/gxrl.

I'm not a man or a woman. Once, I shot an arrow at my best friend, which is to say I've known my share of anger. And I am not a man. I cry watching reality TV. And I am not a woman.

And I won't apologize if that's confusing. Sometimes it is good to get confused like surrealism. Like Claude Cahun's second face in that photograph.

I'm not a man or a woman even in a photograph. Despite what my driver's license or my passport might say. Despite my birth certificate or my draft card, I can't be drafted because you cannot draft what does not exist, and the U.S. army acknowledges only a woman, or better yet, a man.

I'm not a man. I do not pray to a phallic God sitting on his thrown of cock and balls. If I ever choked someone with my penis, I apologize.

But I'm not a woman either. Yes, I have long hair. So did Jesus. And Robert Plant who looked a lot like Farrah Fawcett back in the day.

But I'm not a man. I like to wear short skirts and sheer sleeves. I check out my own ass in the mirror. I carry lipstick in my fanny pack as well as a mini vanity. And I fulfill eleven out of twelve categories in the May 1962 *Vogue* quiz "Are you a 1962 woman?" categories such as: "you wear more than five colors," "you have a job," "you live in air conditioning," and "you wear makeup all day."

But I'm not a woman. Not even from behind. Not even leaning on the bar. You can buy me a drink, but I am not a woman. And I am not a man.

I have kissed a woman. I have kissed a man. I know what they are, but I am not one of them.

There is no section in Kohls or H&M for me. If I didn't know better, I'd think I was supposed to walk around the mall naked like the Garden of Eden where there were no men or women. There was only God and God's creatures, and no one would have been confused by me there.

I'm not a man. Though I get confused with one often. Sometimes my own mother doesn't recognize me. And some people have told me I make them uncomfortable. That I look too much like a woman.

But I'm not a woman, and I think this makes some people think of me as untrustworthy. Sometimes I do not trust myself. I'm not a man or a woman. Though sometimes I tell myself I am. Sometimes I think I am looking for attention or that I am just a liar.

But I'm not a liar. And I'm not a woman or a man. I have fur like any mammal.

I can look fish but don't swim very well. Not Ariel or Poseidon. Though I love to kayak and show off my big arm muscles.

I'm not a woman or a man. I'm a poet and a lover.

And I don't feel any lesser. And I did not get demoted. No one knows what salary to pay me anymore.

Maybe I'm an oak tree. I do like to be still and eat up the sun.

But I'm not what you are thinking. Even in a two piece. Even with a tan that takes your eye all the way up my leg.

Not a woman or a man. Even if you don't believe me. Even if you mistake me for one.

I'm just an egg waiting to be sat on.

Not even when I'm naked am I a woman or a man. Not even in your dreams when you make me stand naked.

Not when shaving my face, my legs. Not during sex in whatever position.

Maybe I'm a red shouldered hawk—like the ones I see high up the longleafs. I think I, too, could balance on the smallest limbs.

Maybe I'm a hymn. A song against binaries: "Holy, holy, holy, merciful and mighty—God in three persons, blessed Trinity."

I'm not a man. And I don't want to be.

I'm not a woman. And I think I'm pretty.

I am a clean slate.

I'm a place for sandwiches to go.

I am a list of microbes.

Just two earlobes and what is in between.

I'm not a _____. I was taught how to be one and it didn't stick.

I'm not a _____. Even if that is the other option you'd give.

I'm not a man or a woman. I never was. Maybe nobody is.

SEXUAL EDUCATION (THE LUTHERAN SCHOOL EDITION)

Sex was sin. So safe was sin.
So why be safe if sent to hell?
Thoughts were sins—think not of thighs.
Looks, as good as lies. Lust
was all there was to us. Weak.
A waste of what the Lord had wanted.
Dreams were sins, like doubts, desires.
Whole genders. God was gracious, to a point.
Lips and legs in heels, long lashes
of course. No condomed cucumber here.
Jive with Jesus not Jezebel.
He might be hot, but hot is hell.
Girls, guide not from God your brothers' gazes.
Your body's a birdhouse of the Blessed Dove.
You are a sinner, a sorrowful sinner.
Now get on your knees and know your God.

"DON'T SAY GAY"

Florida 2022

Say other.
Say problem.
Say sinner.
Say Sodom.
Say Gomorrah.
Say fire.
Say faggot.
Say Hellfire.
Say brimstone.
Say Satan.
Say fallen.
Say pitchfork.
Say pit of fire.
Say furnace.
Say flame.
Say flamer.
Say flamboyant.
Say swish.
Say lisp.
Say suspicious.
Say limp wrist.
Say wide shouldered.
Say stubble.
Say throat.
Say apple.
Say wrong voice.
Say wrong walk.
Say wrong place
between the legs.
Say unnatural.
Say genital.
Say pervert.
Say invert.
Say mama's boy.
Say tomboy.
Say boy boy boy
to a grown woman.
Say good friends.
Say roommates.
Say fad.
Say faze.
Say ahistorical.
Say erase.
Say dead.
Say body.
Say corpse.
Say J[ane]on Doe.
Say blunt force
trauma to the head.
Say found in her bed.
Say found after three days.
Say headline.
Say obit.
Say academic article.
Say theory.
Say Darwin.
Say Natural Selection.
Say biological.
Say animal.
Say extinct species.
Say lesser.
Say lower.
Say on your knees.
Say confession.
Say abomination.
Say fiction.
Say fact.
Say faery.
Say fury.
Say Führer.
Say power.
Say ruler.
Say president.
Say supremacy.
Say hate.
Say legislate.
Say hit.
Say halt.
Say held to the ground.
Say billy club.
Say bullet.
Say in the back.
Say blue.
Say blood.
Say law.
Say order.
Say progress.
Say protest.
Say dissident.
Say undesirable.
Say campaign.
Say concentrate.
Say denial.
Say triangle.
Say ghetto.
Say experiment.
Say camp.
Say solution.

Say what you really mean.

PASTOR/ASSASSIN GHAZAL

You must baptize in your grave. You must die to sin.
Do you want to end up on the devil's BBQ, or fry for sin?

Then, be truthful to a fault. Let yourself be killed.
To tell even a snowflake of a white lie is sin.

Don't lie around on the couch come Sunday. Don't write
bad things about the church. To feel anger or jealousy is sin.

Men, don't look at women unless you have the urge
to look at men (and v/v). Better a claw hammer to the eye than sin.

Don't play Jeopardy with God. Heaven is not a question
as answer. To test your maker, to ask *if* or *why* is sin.

Remember, you're an apple-eater, an Apostle Peter,
a three-times-denier of the Christ, you would deny your sin.

You go by seven deadly names, you are so bad. Chris,
you must die to yourself, or in eternity, you'll die for sin.

THE FUNERAL POEM I WILL NOT BE READING AT MY AUNT BRENDA'S FUNERAL

I won't be reading a funeral poem
at my aunt Brenda's funeral.
I'm not going to the funeral (though maybe I should)
because I live so far away and have little money.

At my aunt Brenda's funeral
there will be no poem
because I live so far away and have little money,
but I think it would please her if

there will be no poem
because she was not one to read poems.
But I think it would please her if
someone read from, say, *The Lord of the Rings.*

Because she was not one to read poems,
I hope they read something else.
Someone could read from, say, *The Lord of the Rings*
because I don't ever remember her reading the Bible.

I hope they read something else,
not that the Bible is bad of course,
but I don't ever remember her reading the Bible.
They could quote from Star Wars. She loved Han Solo.

Not that the Bible is bad. Of course
I want them to mourn and pray, but
they could quote from Star Wars. She loved Han Solo—
how his open vest was sexy, how he shot first, how he was cool.

I want them to mourn and pray, but
talk about her and her life and the man she would have married:
how his open vest would've been sexy, how he'd have shot first and been cool.
I want someone, anyone, saying anything at all about Han Solo.

Talk about her and her life and the man she would have married—
that won't be adequately covered, I think.
I want someone, anyone, saying anything at all about Han Solo
and not reading from the Bible.

She won't be adequately covered, I think,
by a poem
and not reading from the Bible.
Someone needs to say: "You like me because I'm a scoundrel."

By a poem
she would be bored. By this poem.
Someone needs to say: "You like me because I'm a scoundrel,"
so she will not be bored.

She would be bored by this poem
I won't be reading—a funeral poem.
So she will not be bored,
I'm not going to the funeral. Though, maybe I should.

HERETIC

Most centuries, I'd be burned at the stake
like Joan of Arc. Or assassinated,
knifed like Marlowe. At least, I'd get prison
like Galileo. If stargazing's out,
imagine putting the saints in drag. "Witch!
Devil!" they'd cry in torchlight and drag me
off to a pile of sticks leaning 'round
a post—I'd go up like a real faggot.
Murdered for something I said, just like Christ
(I realize, saying that is heresy,
but it's true). When I think of him nailed there
by his wrists for the way he lived, I think
of Matthew Shepard hung on barbed wire. Yes,
I think—write—they still might kill me for this.

THE TOMB

a tanka

An angel came to
the tomb and, knowing, said: "What's
this stone doing here?
Nobody is dead." Their high
heeled foot rolled the stone away.

INTERVIEW WITH THE PUBLIC UNIVERSAL FRIEND

This interview took place in a Rhode Island meeting house formerly associated with The Society of Friends (known otherwise as The Quakers). The meeting house is currently populated by members of The Society of Universal Friends, though it looks much the same as it would have under its previous stewardship—a spare, wood-built building with hard pews where we sat and kneelers without cushions. No cross hangs inside the meeting house, and there is no other decoration to speak of. The interviewee, said to have been reborn in 1776, and known widely as The Public Universal Friend, is a preacher and is held by many to be a prophet. During our interview, The Friend was dressed in loose, black clerical robes and wore a purple kerchief. The preacher wore also a low crowned beaver cap which they removed and hung on the rack after coming in doors. Society members, anxious to listen in on our conversation, had to be dismissed by the preacher before we could begin, and it took much convincing before these followers would believe that no ill will was intended on the part of our paper. Yet, due to the great persuasive power The Friend has over such persons, the matter was finally put to rest. Although some have accused The Friend of deception, blasphemy, apostacy, hysteria, and even outright insanity, their demeaner has been described elsewhere as "decent and graceful and grave," and it is the opinion of this reporter, after having spent some time with The Friend, that they are both eloquent and learned. What follows is an edited version of our interview, taking into mind the main interests of our readers, and in large part stripped of some of the pleasantries that normally begin and intermix such conversations.

Interviewer: Are you a man or a woman?

Public Universal Friend: I am what I am.

Interviewer: And your name?

P.U.F.: The Public Universal Friend.

Interviewer: And you hold that the person who inhabited this body before you is dead?

P.U.F.: Thou sayest it.

Interviewer: And what happened to that person?

P.U.F.: That soul has ascended into heaven. This body has been given a new spirit.

Interviewer: I have read elsewhere that you were suffering a particularly high fever, delirium, is that correct?

P.U.F.: I woke to the fever and the sores.

Interviewer: When you woke, why did you not choose a name like that of others?

P.U.F.: The prophet Isaiah wrote of "a new name which the mouth of the Lord hath named." Mine is a name like unto this.

Interviewer: And your followers all call you by this name?

P.U.F.: Yes. It is my name.

Interviewer: And your followers, they use a kind of neutered language to refer to you otherwise, yes?

P.U.F.: Genderless language, yes.

Interviewer: Yes, a genderless language. They refer to you neither as he nor as she, that is correct?

P.U.F.: Even in their diaries and private correspondences—or so I am told.

Interviewer: And why do you insist on them doing this? Why is it important to you?

P.U.F.: It is important to God who sent me.

Interviewer: And why would God choose someone such as you?

P.U.F.: In Christ we are neither male nor female. We were made in the image of God. And through Christ, we return toward that image.

Interviewer: Why do you think Christ came to earth as a human man then?

P.U.F.: So that people would listen.

Interviewer: Then why do you think God did not send you as a man?

P.U.F.: There will be a day when people are ready to listen not to the body but to the soul.

Interviewer: So you are speaking to a coming generation?

P.U.F.: I speak the word of the Lord which is for every generation.

Interviewer: But you think that perhaps there will be more who will listen in some future generation?

P.U.F.: I do. It is the nature of prophets to be despised in their homelands. Even Christ who is above us all was not accepted in his time in Galilee.

Interviewer: Do you think it would be easier for people to accept your preaching if they were not so confused about whether to call you a man or a woman—he or she?

P.U.F.: Grammar is not the problem. The Society of Friends has long rejected the social ranking implicit in the word "you." We have kept, regardless of rank and class, the common "thee" and "thou" as a protest on our very tongues. What God has asked of me, and all those around me, is no more difficult and no less true.

Interviewer: Is it true that you often do not bring a Bible with you to meetings?

P.U.F.: What was good enough for the prophets of old is good enough for me. I have an excellent memory.

Interviewer: Is it true that a number of former slaves and natives have become regulars at your meetings?

P.U.F.: Just as I would ask not to be précised by the outward appearance of my body, neither would I wish to do this unto another.

Interviewer: Do you believe race, gender, or class to be the greatest issue facing our nation?

P.U.F.: Just as there is no greatest member of the Trinity, there is no one issue that is greatest in America. Each of us is shaped by God and altered by our experience on earth. We are not one thing but many. This is true of the individual and of the nation.

Interviewer: Women hold office in your fellowship, is that correct?

P.U.F.: Yes.

Interviewer: And are they referred to, or are any of the men, as genderless?

P.U.F.: No.

Interviewer: So it is only you? Or are there others like you?

P.U.F.: There are others.

Interviewer: How do you know? Have you met them?

P.U.F.: I have reached countless numbers in spirit. Some have revealed themselves to me here on earth.

Interviewer: How do you reach those you can only reach in spirit?

P.U.F.: Each of us speaks through history—whether in a small, still voice or like an earthquake.

Interviewer: How do you know that people are listening?

P.U.F.: I say what I think is true and is interesting. And I pray.

Interviewer: What would you say to those who might be listening now?

P.U.F.: Thou art true. Thou art an indescribable being.

QUEER JESUS DOESN'T DIE ON A CROSS

Say, that night in Jerusalem, the guards
couldn't find Jesus out in the garden.
Herod went back to his palace. Pilate
got drunk and left the prisoners alone.
The crowd tired, and the Pharisees had
no one to stone. The twelve kept arguing
about who would be the first among them,
and Mary sighed with a mother's relief.
Not one sin of bigotry forgiven.
The temple curtain left intact. The noon
sky undarkened. No crown of thorns. No nails.
And nothing to believe in or condemn
for unbelief. In this new testament,
each one of our Stonewall Saints gets to live.

NOTES

The title of this manuscript is an adaptation of a video title created by the drag performer Gay Jesus.

Latrice Royale is a drag queen who competed in the fourth season of *RuPaul's Drag Race* as well as two seasons of *RuPaul's Drag Race All Stars*. In addition to working as a drag queen, Latrice is also an ordained Christian minister.

The poems "'Now Sissy that Walk' (a Creation Story)," "'We're All Born Naked and The Rest is Drag,'" and "Charisma. Uniqueness. Nerve. & Talent." all borrow their titles (or parts thereof) from phrases coined by RuPaul and made popular in Ru's music and/or on *RuPaul's Drag Race*. Charisma, uniqueness, nerve, and talent are all the attributes a drag queen needs to be successful (as well as a clever acronym).

"Sonnet from the Closet" was originally directly after Candace Williams's "Black Sonnet" and remains formally indebted to that poem.

The title poem "The Drag Gospel of Queer Jesus" takes its form from Christ's Beatitudes.

"Hardtimes Jesus" owes a debt to James Tate's "Good Times Jesus."

In the poem "Burning Haibun for Thomas(ine) Hall's Cross Cloth" I have chosen to use Thomas(ine) most often because Hall went back and forth between the names Thomas and Thomasine during their lifetime. There is not a clear indication which name they preferred (if either). The form of this poem (a burning haibun) was invented by the poet torrin greathouse and is a play on the traditional haibun. The burning haibun consists of a prose poem, then an erasure of that prose poem, and then an erasure of the erasure into a haiku.

"Judas Kissed Me" is after Leigh Hunt's "Jenny Kissed Me."

"Lip Sync (Variation on a Theme by City Girls Ft. Doja Cat)" takes its form from the song "Pussy Talk."

"Hoopoe Ghazal" owes a great debt to Attar's *The Conference of Birds*.

"Davina Cocket: Queen of the Wild Frontier" is after Danez Smith's "Dinosaurs in the Hood."

At Cambridge, Charles Darwin did in fact belong to a student organization known as the Glutton Club, a group devoted to eating "birds and beasts which were before unknown to human palate."

"Anthropofuck" is an invented term derived from 1) Anthropocene: The current geologic era in which human forces began to disproportionately affect the earth and its climate. Some scholars say this period began during the Industrial Revolution, others argue it goes as far back as the beginnings of agriculture. And 2) Genderfuck: A gender expression that purposefully blurs the lines between masc and femme/uses masculine and feminine combinations/rejects femininity and masculinity altogether. A big "fuck you" to the gender binary. A common term in drag culture. This poem also owes a great deal to Etheridge Knight's "Feeling Fucked Up."

"Waters Bop" is a Bop, a form created by Afaa Michael Weaver at the Cave Canem summer retreat.

Of Beargardens: "The Beargarden was a facility for bear-baiting, bull-baiting, and other 'animal sports' in the London area during the 16th and 17th centuries, from the Elizabethan era to the English Restoration period. Baiting is a blood sport where an animal is tormented or attacked by another animal, often dogs, for the purpose of entertainment or gambling."

"Migrations" is in a form which I invented and have given the name "Wild Goose Poem." The form imitates the movements of geese in flight on their long migrations. Each word, like a goose, takes a turn leading the flock/stanza, taking the brunt of the wind. This poem also owes a debt in shape and content to Mary Oliver.

"Apocalypse Narratives" is an adapted form of the curtal sonnet invented by Gerard Manley Hopkins.

"Prayer (I)" by George Herbert, much like my own "Prayer (II)," is a list poem. The end of that list is "something understood" which the reader gets the sense Herbert both believes and disbelieves.

"I'm Not a _____" is after Harold Norse's "I'm Not a Man."

On "Don't Say Gay": "The Parental Rights in Education Act, commonly known by critics as the Don't Say Gay Law, is a Florida law introduced and passed in 2022 which outlined new statutes for primary education, notably for prohibiting classroom instruction on sexual orientation or gender identity from kindergarten to grade 3 in Florida's public school districts, or instruction on sexual orientation or gender identity in a manner that is not 'age appropriate or developmentally appropriate for students' in any grade."

The Public Universal Friend was a real, historical figure and all effort has been made to stay true to their historical existence.

ACKNOWLEDGMENTS

Thanks to the following journals for the initial publications of these poems:

"Apocalypse Narratives," *The Blue Unicorn*

"The Apostle Paula," *Poetry Magazine*

"Burning Haibun for Thomas(ine) Hall's Cross Cloth," *Redivider*

"Charisma. Uniqueness. Nerve. & Talent." *Saw Palm*

"Don't Say Gay," *Saw Palm*

"The Drag Gospel of Queer Jesus," *Wussy*

"At the End of His Life, Nikola Tesla Fell in Love with a Pigeon," *Insert [Brackets]*

"Global Emissions Rose Into the Atmosphere like Emissions Rising Into the Atmosphere," *Only Poems*

"I like to shit in the woods," *Plumwood Mountain Journal*

"Magnificat," *Bosque*

"Migrations," *Prairie Schooner*

"Now Sissy that Walk (a Creation Story)," *Sine Qua Non*

"Prayer (II)," *Frontier Poetry*

"Queer Ecologies (Haiku and Tanka)," *The Harvard Review*

"Sonnet from the Closet," *Wayfarer Magazine*

"The Sonnet in Drag," *Academy of American Poets*

"Stranger," *Cincinnati Review*

"*Waldeinsamkeit*," *Saw Palm*

"We're All Born Naked and the Rest is Drag," *Wayfarer Magazine*

THANKS

All my love, thanks, and joy to my partner, Shannon! You are responsible for the greatest deal of beauty in my life, and without you, living would be a chore.

Thanks to Lady who was and is my heart.

Thanks to my dissertation committee: Molly Hand, JM Kilgore, Virginia Lewis, and especially to L. Lamar Wilson and Cy Weise—y'all helped me bring so many of these poems to life in your classes, and without you this book would not exist.

Thanks to old friends: Chris Green for all your support in my early career, for teaching me about the mystery of poems, and for letting me use your house all those times. Katie LaTour for being my #1 poetry work buddy and Poetry East pal! And to Richard Jones for literally teaching me everything I know about poems. Without you, I wouldn't even know which way to hold a pencil.

Thanks to my friends at Apalachicola Riverkeeper, and particularly Georgia Ackerman and Cam Baxley for all the work you have done protecting my favorite place! And thanks to all the water protectors and stewards of the more-than-human world!

Thanks to Dani Davis for being the only person I know crazy enough to do all our swamp stomps and paddles which were invaluable to this book!

Thanks to all the cohort friends who kept me going, especially River Selby and Sáannii (Tacey) M. Atsitty!

Thanks to the friends who kept me in conversation throughout the writing process: Lily and Noah Winn-Calzado, Aaron Stearns, (Father) Greg Kasen, and especially to Liesel and Ryan Hamilton, my constant companions in book chatter and bird talk.

Thanks to my editor, Sarah Wetzel, who has made countless invaluable suggestions and trusted my insanity, and to all the Saturnalia staff!

And special thanks to Jackie Farley who, more than anyone, waded through the numerous drafts that became this book. Thank you, friend!

Thanks to my sibling, Beth, for all of your love and support, and for being who I wanted to be when I grew up, and to my sister-in-law, Jackie Price for literally being the coolest person I know.

Thank you to my parents, Angie and Wayne, for loving me through the weird times and for keeping me alive when things could have gone otherwise. And thank you for always filling our house with books and music.

Thank you to my grandparents, Lee and Donna, for being two of the greatest people I know on the planet earth.

Thanks to all the queer and trans writers who came before me and to the whole queer community.

And thanks to anyone reading this book. That's very cool of you because I worked very hard on it.

BIO

Chrysanthemum (Chris) Brook Watkins is a trans poet, writer, and environmental activist living in North Florida. They spend as much time as they can on the water and in the swamps and are a proud board member of Apalachicola Riverkeeper. Chris received her PhD in Poetry with a focus in ecopoetics and environmental writing, poetic forms, and queer literature from Florida State University. Chris now works as the Academics and Partnerships Coordinator at FSU's Office of Sustainability (Sustainable Campus) and teaches both writing and sustainability courses. Some of her newer essays and poems (not included in this book) can be found in *Ecotone*, *Terrain.org*, and *The Dodge* among other journals.

If you were moved by the words found here, consider giving to Apalachicola Riverkeeper or another water protection group/steward of the more-than-human world, without whom many of these poems would not be possible. Support trans people and all queers!

The Drag Gospel of Queer Jesus was printed in Adobe Caslon
www.saturnaliabooks.org

www.ingramcontent.com/pod-product-compliance
Lightning Source LLC
LaVergne TN
LVHW080332110826
845155LV00024B/150

* 9 7 8 1 9 4 7 8 1 7 9 6 8 *